G000065877

Unlocking the Brilliant Mind

1st Edition

Table of Contents

Fair use policy

This book contains a small number of "no more than is required" quotes and common proverbs that are centuries old, used fairly, intended for critique and review, and are accompanied by sufficient acknowledgement to the author, where known.

Introduction

Who I am

My name is Stephanie Scanlan-Georgescu, and I am a qualified hypnotherapist and MSC public health consultant with a working history of managing corporate teams and processes within public affairs and Chief of Staff divisions.

Personal Therapy

I am also the founder of Wave Therapy Clinic, where I specialise in person therapy techniques such as CBT and hypnotherapy.

I have assisted many clients in coping with work-related stress and chronic fatigue syndrome, that is often misunderstood, hard to diagnose and can often lead to poor performance in all areas of life, if not treated. Similarly, I have helped ease the severity of those suffering with differing types of trauma, such as grievance and nervous shock and I have had good success in helping those with speech and confidence challenges to become more confident in the spoken word and expression.

Motivation

Using my experience, I wanted to write a book that would help people unlock their powers within, by coaching them to achieve brilliance in a time of crisis.

Having experience with unlocking the subconscious mind of others, I wanted to share some of the tools that have helped me create instant positive lasting change with people from all walks of life and in numerous settings.

Tools

This book provides an easy to digest set of tools that will help anyone build a more robust and healthier mindset.

Some of my tools include **metaphors disguised as quotes, proverbs, breathing exercises, energy management techniques** and the like.

Philosophers, from the Buddha, Aristotle, and Plato to more modern psychoanalysts, understood that the answers we seek to a happier life lay hidden deep within the depths of our unconscious minds, in some form or other.

The Power of Metaphors disguised as quotes

Many mid-20th century psychoanalysts often invented clever metaphors, sometimes disguised as quotes, to help heal the afflictions of their patients.

Transcendental language has long been used to encourage behavioural change in patients making significant impacts in the field of psychotherapy.

Some would often term the process as: "magical".

Why uncertainty impedes our happiness

Many theorists share the view that we, as humans, have a basic set of needs that we seek to fulfil, and once complete, we become obsessed with finding higher needs to fulfil.

Needs can vary and can be plentiful. Often when we are in a state of uncertainty, we look outside for quick fixes that rarely provide us with what we really need.

The need to fulfil our needs

The depth of our search is dependent on the need we are trying to fulfil and the likelihood of obtainment.

When we are unable to achieve such needs, we often turn to instant gratification that sets us down the path of unhealthy choices.

Why we make unhealthy choices

Those unhealthy choices can range from vast quantities of alcohol, fast foods, toxic relationships and, in the more extreme cases, drugs and illegal behaviours.

However, there comes a point when the quick fixes no longer work, which is often the point where depression, anger or anxiety can attack us at our weakest points.

It is in this state where our search becomes amplified, as we are now operating within a destructive mindset.

The sliding scale of doom

OK - So maybe your life is not all that doom and gloom as I have described it to be, but it is worth thinking about.

Many hypnotherapists believe that everyone is on a spectrum.

On the one end, we have those that seek minor gratifications, and on the other, those that seek major gratifications which will get them into trouble.

Some psychologists, psychoanalysts and hypnotherapists believe that the only thing that separates us from our own destruction is our ability to resist major gratifications, that will lead us down that garden path.

And it is at the bottom of that path, where true unhappiness resides.

Awakening the entrepreneur within us

The market

For many, uncertainty makes us confused and frustrated. However, many technology, home essentials and improvement, remote fitness, and pharma companies have seen a huge surge in profit due to this pandemic, because of increased home working.

The self

This means there is an opportunity for innovation, and it is a great time to think about a starting a new business venture.

Start-ups do require money, but there are options for funding, including crowd funding, that can help one get up and running.

There is even room for the everyday person to explore new business ideas - in the home essentials and home fitness categories.

The future

Similarly, post this pandemic, people will be reflecting on their experiences, which will see the invention of some interesting artistic interpretations, as has happened post wars.

We may also see a surge in specific educational courses, from resilience and crisis management to shorter courses in public health, pharma, public relations, arts and crafts and all things communication, as a by-product of increased political awareness and increased access to technology across the globe.

This means that there is also an opportunity to learn and acquire new skills, that will make us more employable in the growing age of communication.

The aim and purpose of this book

This book is for everyone and anyone that wants to achieve brilliance.

The purpose of this book is to help others break unhealthy cycles that can often lead to failure.

However, it should not be taken lightly that even when one is on that path of success, there is great benefit from engaging our minds in positive mental simulations.

This book seeks to gently remove those unwanted thoughts that are blocking our paths to success, by reframing our internal mind chatter with positive life changing commitments.

How to use this book

On each page you will find a number of tools, including **quotes/metaphors, proverbs, breathing exercises, visualisation exercises**, and more, that will encourage you to search within, helping to bring forth the positive answers you seek, or to rid your mind of senseless chatter.

All you need to do is read, then follow the explanations or instructions to help you reflect on the meaning or task.

2 happiness exercises

Included in this book, there are 2 happiness exercises to help you measure your progression throughout this journey.

4 reflections to consider

There are 4 reflections that should not be rushed, and it is advised that you take your time to see how they relate to you.

2 proverbs to consider

There are 2 proverbs that you should take your time to read and internalise so that you see how they might relate to you.

2 breathing exercises

These can be done at any time, but it is advisable that you do the first one early, to help reduce any existing stress before you continue to read.

Visualisation exercise

This can be done at any time, but should be done before the affirmations section.

Orientations

These are specifically crucial as they may reveal different aspects of the self, and provide practical steps to help you do this. However, the dietary orientation can be done alongside reading this book. (page 67)

Overall guidance

It is the practical considerations of each tool, that will guide you in your exploration of the mind, by helping you to extract meaning that will create lasting brilliance.

Remember: **You are the architect of your inner and outer world, and the brilliance is within you already!**

Acknowledgments

Thank you to my husband *Mihai Georgescu* for staying up with me late at night, keeping me refreshed with food and sustenance and feeding me with brilliant ideas.

Thank you to my cats for never failing to keep up their demands on my time whilst writing this book.

This book is also dedicated to several of my former clients and colleagues, who persevered with me long enough for me to help them unlock their own brilliance.

Scaling your happiness

Technology is helping us to become more connected than ever before, therefore mental health and well-being strategies have become more popular and measurable as the world has evolved.

Well-being has a dual benefit

Across the world, companies are investing in well-being activities to improve employee happiness, because an absence of employee happiness often leads to huge financial deficits for businesses.

This means that a shared benefit exists between employers and employees, as employees want to feel happier, and employers want to avoid loss of revenue.

One of the challenges with these well-being improving activities, is that happiness is very intangible and subjective to each individual, and is often influenced by the uncertain and everchanging environment.

There are many skills-based quizzes that one can do online to measure happiness.

However, to get you started, I have devised a starter reflection activity:

On a scale of 1-10, can you say how happy you are?

Mark the line below to indicate where you think you score between 1 and 10, so we can revisit this section later.

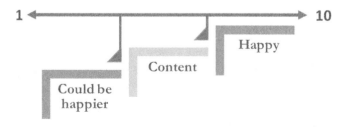

Reflections of the Buddha

Three things cannot be
long hidden:
The sun
The moon
The truth.

The Buddha teaches us that the truth lies within.

Sometimes, before we can move forward, we need to take some time to consider the thoughts and behaviours that we want to keep and those that we want to rid ourselves of.

The diagnosis

This is a kind of diagnosis, in that before we can adapt to new ways of thinking, we first need to know what thoughts or feelings might be holding us back.

For many, as simple as this might seem, it can be quite a challenging task, and it is the avoidance of this question that can hinder our progress.

Note! – Use the space below to write the thoughts and/or behaviours that you wish to keep or rid yourself of!

1.

2.

3.

4.

5.

6.

Reflections of Aristotle

It is the mark of an
educated mind to be
able to entertain a
thought without
accepting it.

Aristotle

Aristotle was a Greek philosopher that made important contributions to society, around how we now perceive logic and reason.

For Aristotle, thoughts alone did not make a person logical, however it was the commitment to that thought where the true logic resided.

Is that thought healthy?

Knowing what thoughts and behaviours we want to keep or reject, allows us to truly reflect about the commitment to our thoughts.

For instance: What thoughts serve our purpose to move forward, and what thoughts do not?

Example: I want that job, but my mind tells me I am not good enough for that role, or that I am a qualification short of experience. Do I accept this this thought, or *do I just ignore it like a bad cloud passing over the sky, and continue to pursue that job?*

Getting rid of unwanted thoughts

Every thought that one has from now on should be considered, before accepting or rejecting.

A thought should only be accepted on the basis that it supports our cause in seeking brilliance. This is the essential Aristotelian basis for logical reasoning.

Our unconscious minds will often hold sadness from past and/or forgotten memories. Those forgotten memories can often manifest and resurface in ways sometimes one cannot describe.

Nevertheless, this quote reminds us that we are the true masters of our feelings and that we do not have to accept unwanted emotions, that no longer serve our well-being.

Concentrating on the positives

Newfound research also suggests that concentrating on positives can help us move forward without taking our minds back to that negative place that made us feel unhappy.

30

Interlude

We can conclude that, to reach a balanced state of consideration where we make logical decisions, it is necessary to release all thought that blocks our paths to brilliance.

We can also conclude that sadness is only a state of mind. Our minds are so neuroplastic (malleable) that if we convince ourselves often enough that we are happy, then we will become happy. *We are, after all, what we eat and the words we think!*

Reflections of Plato

Better a little which is well done, than a great deal imperfectly.

Plato

Plato was a Greek Philosopher and was of the view that a good life requires more than just expert knowledge, but also required healthy emotional and harmony between the three parts of the soul, including reason, spirit, and appetite.

<u>Dangers of consumerism</u>

The media and advertisers know all too well that the human loves a quick fix, where capitalism drives that ever-increasing pressure to buy more, spend more, do more and get more done.

But getting more done does not necessarily fulfil a particular need nor does it lead to the production of quality.

In such chaos and in the pursuit of obtainment, we very often forget that it is better to do less but well, than more and imperfectly. Therefore, it is no wonder we have become confused and lost in all this chaos.

Adjusting our pace

This quote echoes to us that, before we can start to master brilliance, we first need to consider at what pace we are moving at, and whether there is a need and scope to adjust.

Having spare capacity

Having some spare capacity allows us to think more considerably about the steps we want to take, which helps us to make calculated moves through life.

The fittest person can indeed run faster, but it is the wise person that knows the road.

A breathing exercise

To help us reset the pace and quieten our minds, sometimes it is good to practice breathing.

Guidance: Read the below before practicing on your own. (Disclaimer: Not to be done whilst driving, or near any machinery!)

Finding a quiet spot

Find yourself a quiet spot, where you will not be interrupted.

Finding the right music

Choose some slow and relaxing quiet songs or a playlist, preferably without words, that plays for at least 30 minutes.

Take 10 minutes to breath in and out, closing your eyes and relaxing your muscles, so they feel deep and heavy. Try to imagine nothing but the sounds of the song.

Sitting or lying flat

Say to yourself:

"I am relaxing and thinking of nothing but the sounds of the song."

Then just relax and let the songs play out for as long as you need.

When the songs end, say to yourself:

"I am now feeling really light and airy as if I am day-dreaming on a cloud in the sky"

When you feel it is time, open your eyes and tell yourself that you have done a good job.

You should then be feeling energised and refreshed to start on your journey to complete whatever it is that you desire.

Orientation: are we thinking right or left

Many hypnotherapists believe that we either think with the right side of the brain or left side of the brain.

The right side of the brain

The right side of the brain is seen as being in charge of thinking that is less organised. The following may have their origin in this side: (not an exhaustive list)

- Being intuitive

- Being imaginative

- Being artistic and having rhythm

- Thinking holistically

- Understanding nonverbal language

- Thinking in an unorganised fashion

- Thinking outside the box

- Thinking in a free-spirited fashion

The left side of the brain

Contrastingly, the left side of the brain is seen as being more organized, and it is thought that the following thinking processes (not an exhaustive list) might originate from this side:

- Being able to compute Language

- Being able to problem solve

- Being logical

- Being able to compute math

- Thinking laterally

Undertaking some research

There are many personality tests and books online, that will help you figure out what side of the brain you use more of.

Many people are a combination of the two!

Balancing of the minds

The trick to a balanced mind is to work out which side is weaker, so we can work on brain training exercises to strengthen the weaker side.

For example, if one wants to be more logical and mathematical, then practicing math's quizzes and logical reasoning exercises will help.

Equally, if one wants to sharpen their right side of the brain, then engaging in artistic activities can be helpful too.

Reflections of Confucius

Success depends upon previous preparation, and without such preparation there is sure to be failure.

Confucius

Confucius was a Chinese Philosopher of great stature and was clearly very tall, however his height in historical accounts varies widely from 6 foot to 9 foot.

Confucius considered education and reflective thought as good practice for those seeking to lead and really sowed the seeds for leadership in early Chinese culture.

He was known for rising-up the ranks quickly, taking many odd jobs, later becoming the Criminal Minister of Lu using his many talents.

Confucius's journey teaches us that success normally comes from the building blocks and baby steps we make in life.

Just like Confucius, many of us have had to take the odd job to make ends meet, which may have felt like a contradiction and backstep towards our future goals and plans.

Odd jobs

However, Confucius also reminds us that all steps regardless of job, are merely the preparation for the real thing. It is amazing what transferable skills can be learnt from any job or task in life!

Seeing value in everything we do

The key is to see the value in everything we do, and how that can support us in our next adventure, whatever that might be.

Another perspective is that preparation is key. No matter how clever one is, if one does not prepare adequately and does not do their research or takes shortcuts, then one is bound to fall short.

This is particularly key with job interviews.

Revising for an interview

A tactic, I have heard more frequently from clients and colleagues, is that one should revise for an interview 1 level down, their own level and 1 level up. This ensures that you can meet your interviewer at their level, as one cannot assume their interviewers will be as well-versed in the subject matter as you!

Similarly, another tactic that I have heard from colleagues is to revise broadly, so that you avoid being bottlenecked or faced with questions that one cannot answer.

A well-known Chinese proverb

A conversation with a wise person is better than 10 year' of study.

We know that we are what we eat, and we are what we think. Therefore, it makes sense that we are also the company we keep, in the most practical sense.

We can never underestimate what a wise person can teach us that we may not be able to teach ourselves.

This is true of many of the ancient arts including martial arts, where the Sifu passes down ancient knowledge that you will not find in any textbook.

Finding an opportunity to connect

There is an opportunity here to seek out coaches, mentors, leaders, elders, and those that will be able to pass down some invaluable knowledge that will help you towards achieving brilliance.

Why would we try to recreate the wheel when we know someone has already created it before?

Choosing wisely

This proverb also teaches us to be more observant with the company we keep, by occasionally assessing whether any relationship we are engaging in helps us to achieve happiness and brilliance.

After all, we do want to be the best versions of ourselves, and having friends and colleagues that do so too, is the ultimate bonus to our happiness.

A well-known Chinese proverb

Skills can never be one's burden.

The market: innovation vs exploration

The need to keep up with learning in this constantly evolving environment, is ever-growing.

Many businesses must be innovative, and they often have to look outside the company to see what the market is doing and how market trends might affect their services or products. This means learning something new is almost always guaranteed, regardless of company structure.

However, *companies with more of a functional structure concentrate on looking at internal skillsets.* For instance, instead of learning something new, functional structure companies find ways to improve and develop their existing skills and talents.

The self: innovation vs exploration

Companies have their own identities like people, which is why we are often faced with the same challenge of *whether to brush-up on our existing knowledge by exploring and sharpening our skill set, or whether to seek new skills to be innovative.*

This proverb motivates us to have that very conversation with ourselves frequently, so that we can stay afloat in this highly competitive market.

54

Learning does not come cheap, however, in this growing age of communication, one can now find high-quality free online courses, or courses that have payments plans for those with a tight budget.

Being stuck in a dead-end job provides us with an opportunity to either improve on an existing skill or to seek innovative skills that can build confidence.

Maybe that new skill might just land us that new job, taking us from dead end to high-end!

Managing our energy

Many hypnotherapists, including myself, know that there is more to therapy than just the sessions.

Many clients will also have homework to do, because being healthy in every sense must come from within.

It is no surprise that the number 1 recurring theme that many clients share is the absence of energy.

Energy depletes throughout the day, but at night, our dreams are there to remove those stresses away, so we can start afresh the following day.

However, if we are feeling tired and/or exhausted, then it means that we are not using our own energy efficiently.

Time management

Time never stops, and with only 24 hours in a day, it is important that we are good with managing our time efficiently and effectively.

There are several things that we can do to manage our energies more efficiently, which have proved successful and **are published within many "well-being circles" that you can find on any online search.**

I have included some tailored well-being suggestions below, which I have used in therapeutic practice.

Physical

Getting at least 8 hours sleep every night is crucial to our survival and can help us ***gain more energy.***

Poor sleep is the number 1 factor of tiredness. Therefore, it is important to eat healthy, limit alcohol intake and to exercise as often as one can.

Psychological

Ways in which to ***preserve energy*** comes from avoiding conflict at all costs and engaging

58

in well-being exercises that help us to feel relaxed like swimming, tai-chi, and yoga.

Sometimes we cannot avoid conflict, therefore looking at things from a different perspective can help us to develop a healthy level of empathy for the situation.

Sometimes expanding the mind and dipping our heads into a book can provide us with a certain level of recuperative escapism.

Societal

In the current crisis, social isolation has made it harder for us to interact with other human beings. However, as we are social beings, it is important that we avoid loneliness at all costs, as it can lead to depression which **_depletes our_**

energy.

Sometimes loneliness can happen by accident and before we know it, we feel isolated. Similarly, loneliness can also be formed by accidental habit.

To avoid forming a loneliness habit, we should take every opportunity to stay in touch with friends, family, colleagues, companions, and anyone that makes us feel happy, including getting out in the open air, as much as we can.

However, for some of us, having someone to reach out to might not be an option, and in that case, it might be useful to consider if having a pet would fill that gap, as pets make brilliant companions.

Emotional

Research shows that we are happier when we have purpose.

Taking the time out to listen to a stranger, a friend or colleague without passing judgment or offering advice, can be **_energisingly rewarding._**

Equally, having positive interactions with persons with mental health disabilities can also be **_immensely beneficial and engergising_** for them in the current climate.

Spiritual

Sometimes we need a higher purpose to **keep us motivated and energised.** Therefore, seeking adventures that really make us feel that we are alive, or that we are making a difference, can be good for the soul.

See a list of activities to consider below. (In accordance with current restrictions only)

- Creating a new schedule to become more technologically organised

- Finding a new hobby or learning a new skill

- Finding a cause to champion

- Find ways to contribute to public health research

- Giving to a local cause

- Giving to an international cause

- Giving blood

- Helping a local homeless person

- Participating in a local and national consultation – have your say!

- Starting up a new business venture

- Supporting a friend, family member or work colleague in need

- Volunteering in a chosen charity or homeless person's shelter

A visualisation exercise

To help us focus on our goals, sometimes it is good to practice visualising - what it is that we want to achieve.

Guidance: Read the following before practicing on your own. (Disclaimer: Not to be done whilst driving, or near any machinery)

Finding a quiet spot

Find yourself a quiet spot, where you will not
be interrupted.

Finding the right music

Choose some nice slow relaxing quiet songs or
a playlist, preferably without words, that plays
for at least 15 minutes.

Take 5 minutes to breath in and out closing
your eyes and relaxing your muscles, so they
feel deep and heavy. Try to imagine nothing
but the sounds of the song.

Visualise

Say to yourself when you are ready:

"I am going to relax and visualise the things that I desire"

Then just relax and let the songs play out, and when you are ready, say to yourself:

"I am now relaxed and feeling ready to tackle my desires with passion and enthusiasm."

Opening your eyes when you are ready.

You should then be feeling determined to tackle whatever it is that you desire.

An orientation exercise

This is now an opportunity for us to think about our lifestyle and whether it supports our road to happiness.

Below are 8 working day weekly grids, where you can record your daily food and drink intake, to see if your diet could be improved.

As a qualified public health specialist, I can say that studies show that eating a balanced diet provides sufficient energy needed, helping us to avoid physical fatigue and or exhaustion.

Tips for this exercise!

Think about what could be changed immediately to suit a healthy diet for you.

Look online for some healthy tips around nutritional foods that will help give you more natural energy.

It might be a good idea to take stock now, so that you can see measurable change.

You might like to weigh yourself, and or you may want to observe the changes in the skin and hair by taking a picture before you start the exercise.

	Breakfast	Lunch	Dinner	Alcohol intake
Mon				
Tues				
Wed				
Thurs				
Fri				

	Breakfast	Lunch	Dinner	Alcohol intake
Mon				
Tues				
Wed				
Thurs				
Fri				

	Breakfast	Lunch	Dinner	Alcohol intake
Mon				
Tues				
Wed				
Thurs				
Fri				

	Breakfast	Lunch	Dinner	Alcohol intake
Mon				
Tues				
Wed				
Thurs				
Fri				

	Breakfast	Lunch	Dinner	Alcohol intake
Mon				
Tues				
Wed				
Thurs				
Fri				

	Breakfast	Lunch	Dinner	Alcohol intake
Mon				
Tues				
Wed				
Thurs				
Fri				

	Breakfast	Lunch	Dinner	Alcohol intake
Mon				
Tues				
Wed				
Thurs				
Fri				

	Breakfast	Lunch	Dinner	Alcohol intake
Mon				
Tues				
Wed				
Thurs				
Fri				

	Breakfast	Lunch	Dinner	Alcohol intake
Mon				
Tues				
Wed				
Thurs				
Fri				

Use the section below to note your

observations!

Becoming more resilient

The recent crisis has increased our frequency of using technology, blurring the lines between work and homelife, via the use of new video-based communication tools.

Many believe that the time to improve on our resilience has come.

I have included some techniques below, that will be useful in building a strong mindset to get one through the difficult times.

1. Accepting the things that cannot be changed, but changing the things that can

2. Avoiding acting on impulse

3. Becoming more assertive by learning to say no and push back politely

4. Admitting when you have made a mistake, which can help to build trust and respect

5. Building confidence so that is easier to handle rejection and/or non-constructive feedback

6. Being authentic, as people are more open to authenticity

7. Cutting down on screen time

8. Developing a strong social network of people that support you

9. Developing leadership and management skills to foster team trust

10. Developing decision-making skills to avoid anxiety overload

11. Developing problem-solving skills, making problems feel lighter on the mind

12. Developing cooperation skills and admitting that you need help

13. Establishing goals that keep you focused on the path to brilliance

14. Finding a work-life balance that works for you

15. Following maps when travelling, to avoid getting lost

16. Following written instructions to avoid making mistakes

17. Identifying your blind spots

18. Identifying your skill gaps

19. Identifying your triggers

20. Practicing relaxation techniques to reduce stress

21. Learning an invaluable skill that everyone needs

22. Practicing saving money for a rainy day, as having surplus funds can get you through the hard times

23. Practicing affirmations

24. Practicing persuasion skills, helping others to be more agreeable with you

25. Reflecting on past mistakes and learning from them

26. Scheduling time for fun

27. Taking time out to frequently recharge your batteries

28. Trying to see the bigger picture to get a broader insight into challenges

29. Using a coach/mentor/hypnotherapist to help you develop a strong mind-set

An intermediate breathing exercise

It is good to practice more advanced techniques of breathing, so that we can empty the daily stresses from our minds.

Guidance: read the below before practicing on your own. (Disclaimer: Not to be done whilst driving, or near any machinery)

Finding a quiet spot

Find yourself a quiet spot, where you will not be interrupted.

Finding the right music

Choose some slow relaxing quiet songs or a playlist, preferably without words, that plays for at least 20 minutes.

Take 10 minutes to breath in and out closing your eyes and relaxing your muscles, so they feel deep and heavy. Try to imagine nothing but the sounds of the song.

Lying flat and counting down

Facing the ceiling, try to **concentrate on any spot of your choice, counting down from 20 to 1**, slowly, closing your eyes when you are ready.

When you get to 1, say to yourself:

"I am going to relax and think of nothing but the sounds of the song."

Then just relax and let the songs play out for as long as you need.

When you are ready, say to yourself:

"I am relaxed and refreshed and am ready to count myself back up."

Counting up

Then just count from 1 to 20, opening your eyes when you are ready.

You should then be feeling refreshed and reset to start whatever it is that you desire to do.

Making affirmations

The difference between affirmations and visualisations

Unlike visualising, which we often do semi-consciously and often in a relaxed state, like daydreaming for instance; affirmations are conscious promises made to oneself that help to reframe the way we see things by shifting our negative thoughts to more positive thoughts. Affirmations (also referred to as mantras) can also provide us with direction so that we can avoid self-sabotaging.

Sometimes thinking up those lengthy affirmations can be challenging on top of our

88

daily stresses. Therefore, I have created some affirmations that are commonly used around the world, to help you get started.

Affirmations (in accordance with current restrictions only)

Morning

- Today is going to be a great day, and I am grateful for being alive

- Today I will do something that has meaning to myself and others

- Today I am going to avoid negative habits

- Today I am going to avoid toxic relationships

- Today I am going to venture out so that I can top-up on my vitamin D

- Today I am doing to relax and do nothing because I am always doing something

- Today I am going to learn a new skill

- Today I am going to stop procrastinating, by doing that positive thing that I have been putting off for a while

Afternoon

- Starting from tomorrow, I am going to take regular breaks from my work desk

- Starting from tomorrow, I am going to take a walk around the park to get some fresh air

- Starting from tomorrow, I am going to eat a healthy lunch

- Starting from tomorrow, I am going to call friends or family

Night

- Starting from tomorrow, I am going to get an early night

- Starting from tomorrow, I am going to reduce my caffeine intake

- Starting from tomorrow, I am going to eat a healthy dinner

- Starting from tomorrow, I am going to read a great book

- Starting from tomorrow, I am going to read an educational book

- Starting from tomorrow, I am going to take time to reflect on my actions from the day before

<u>Your affirmations</u>

Use the space below to add your own
affirmations for morning, noon, and night!

- 1.

- 2.

- 3.

- 4.

- 5.

- 6.

Scaling your happiness

Just before you go, do take the time to consider your current state of happiness, by marking the line below as you did earlier on. Has your happiness score improved? (compare with your previous score)

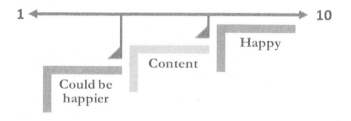

Well done!

Well done for successfully completing this book and investing in your future.

Printed in Great Britain
by Amazon

61179249R00058